Scout Games

A collection of more than 50 scout games

James K. Mercaldo
Chris T. Mercaldo

Printed in the United States.
First Printing
National Edition

Aquinas Scout Fun Books
c/o Thomas C. Mercaldo
154 Herbert Street
Milford, CT 06461
(203) 876-2822

Aquinas Scout Fun Books is not officially affiliated with the Boy Scouts of America, Girl Scouts of America, Scouts Canada or the World Organization of Scouting.

Scout Fun Books can be purchased on a wholesale basis for resale in Camp Stores, Scout Shops and Trading Posts. For details write to us at the above address or contact us by email at BoyScoutBooks@aol.com.

Preface

In his later years, James Naismith talked about how the game of basketball came to be. "The invention of basketball was not an accident. It was developed to meet a need. Those boys simply would not play 'drop the neckerchief' any longer."

Every week, Scoutmasters face the same challenge Naismith faced. There will be Scouts that participate in Scouting primarily because Scouting is fun, so offering an active game period at every Scout meeting is critical to bringing boys back week after week. Coming up with stimulating game ideas is not always easy, though. Some units have limited space in their meeting halls, or need games for very small or very large numbers of youth. The Scout Games book is designed to help Scoutmasters deliver meeting fun regardless of the challenges any unit may face. This includes: active games; traditional games; indoor games; outdoor games; games suited for youth of varied ages; heights and weights; games for large groups; and games for small groups. There are many options to help solve the diverse problems a leader might face. Even games designed to reinforce Scouting skills like knot tying and first aid are included. Some of these games originated with Baden Powell and are time tested, while other games are more contemporary. They are all Scout tested and guaranteed to deliver fun. Games are rated with between one and five stars. Five-star games are the best and most popular with Scouts, while one-star games are enjoyable but are generally suited for a particular purpose. We hope that you enjoy this collection of Scout games and that they help you deliver an outstanding program.

Tom Mercaldo

4

Table of Contents

Field and Outdoor Games

Small Meeting Hall Games

Poison ★ ★ ★ ★

Type: Indoor / Outdoor / Active / Boy Scout / Cub Scout / Large Group / Small Group / Small Space
Equipment: none

Draw or tape a circle on the floor (generally around 6 feet in diameter, but larger or smaller depending on the number of Scouts). Scouts join hands making a complete circle. Everyone begins moving rapidly around the circle without letting go of the person next to them, all the while trying to force Scouts on either side of them to step into the circle. Any Scout who steps into the circle is poisoned and either he or his patrol receives a point. The Scout or patrol with the lowest number of points at the end of the game is the winner.

Variation 1: Scouts poisoned three times are eliminated. Last 5 or 6 Scouts are declared the winners.

Variation 2: Three or more empty, 2 liter soda bottles are arranged on the floor at various points equal distances apart (e.g. in the form of an equilateral triangle, square or pentagon). The Scouts form a circle around these, each Scout using his right hand to grip his neighbor's left wrist. Thus, if the circle breaks the Scoutmaster can instantly see who let go. The object of the game is to pull another Scout into one of the bottles so they will knock it over. The Scout who lets go or knocks over a bottle is out of the game. When only three or four are left the game becomes quite challenging.

Potato ★ ★ ★ ★

Type: Indoor / Moderate / Traditional / Boy Scout / Small Group / Small Space
Equipment: neckerchiefs or blindfolds

Scouts close their eyes or place neckerchiefs over their eyes and slowly walk around trying to avoid other Scouts. Whenever they bump into another player they whisper "Sorry" and continue on. The Scoutmaster secretly chooses one of the Scouts to be the potato. Whenever this player bumps into someone they whisper "Potato" and the player who was bumped into must step out and stand against the wall. Play continues until only the potato and one player remain.

Snake Wall – Fire Wall ★ ★ ★ ★

Type: Indoor / Active / Boy Scout / Cub Scout / Small Group / Large Group / Small Space / Large Space
Equipment: none

The game is played in a room with two walls opposite each other that are relatively free of any obstacles. The game begins with Scouts lined up along one of the walls. The Scout leader clearly identifies each wall to the Scouts, one wall being called the snake wall and the other wall being the fire wall. When the wall is called out, the Scouts need to run to the appropriate wall as quickly as possible. The last one to touch the wall is out. The Scout leader can call out the name of the wall where the Scouts are currently standing and catch Scouts that leave their position if they are the last to return.

Indian Leg Wrestling ★ ★ ★

Type: Indoor / Moderate / Small Space / Traditional / Boy Scout / Small Group / Large Group / Small Area
Equipment: none

This is a trial of skill between two Scouts. Scouts lie on their backs side-by-side in opposite directions. Each Scout grasps the other Scout's shoulder. Aloud they count to three to start, or start on the Scoutmaster's commands. On the first and second count, opponents each lift their inside leg up to a vertical position meeting the leg of the opponent. On the third count they vigorously lock legs and attempt to roll the other Scout up onto their shoulders. There are techniques involved and the biggest or strongest Scout does not always win.

Indian Arm Wrestling ★★★

Type: Indoor / Moderate / Small Space / Traditional / Boy Scout / Small Group
Equipment: none

This is a game of skill between two Scouts. The Scouts place their right feet side by side. Each Scout then grabs his opponent's right wrist with his right hand. The objective is to get the other Scout to move his right foot. Scouts may move their left foot freely, shift weight, or pull and push the other Scout with his right arm. The left arm cannot be used to push or pull. The first Scout to get his opponent to lose his balance and move his right foot wins.

Garret's Game ★★★★

Type: Indoor / Moderate / Small Space / Cub Scout / Boy Scout / Large Group / Small Group / Patrol Competition
Equipment: one tennis ball, barriers forming a rectangular area

This game was designed by the troop of one of the contributing author's for use in small meeting halls where there isn't a lot of space. The objective of the game is to eliminate all the players on the other team. A playing area is defined typically by taking folding tables and turning them sideways to form a "walled in" area. The "walls" do not need to be at a 90 degree angle to the floor. Scouts are broken up into two teams typically of 4 to 8 players. A Scout must throw the ball off a wall and have it bounce on the ground at least once before hitting an opponent to get him out. It may bounce multiple times but it must bounce at least once. A player is not eliminated if he catches the ball. Scouts can accidently eliminate themselves or teammates if they are hit on a bounce and do not catch it. If the ball leaves the playing area, the person who threw it is out. The team that eliminates all of their opponent's players wins.

Knot Relay ★★★

Type: Indoor / Outdoor / Moderate / Cub Scouts / Boy Scouts / Small Groups / Large Group / Small Area / Relay / Patrol Competition
Equipment: small lengths of rope (best if one per Scout, but minimum one per team), staff or pole

Instruct patrols or groups to sit in relay-style lines facing a judge. Place the pole or staff horizontally next to the judge. Give each Scout a length of rope that he can tie knots with. On a signal, the first Scout in each line must run up to the judge, tie the first knot on a list and return to tag the next person in line. Upon being tagged, the next Scout runs up and ties the next knot. For example, the first Scout in each group has to tie a square knot, and then the second Scout in each group has to tie a timber hitch, and so on. This continues until the patrol successfully ties each knot on the list. The first group to tie all of the knots wins. If a Scout ties the knot wrong he can run back to the group and return to try again or, alternatively, the next group member in line can run up and attempt tie the knot.

Variation 1: Make a set time and see which group can complete as many of the same knots within the given time. With this variation, groups do not have to be adjusted based on size. Incorrectly tied knots do not count towards the total. Time should be enough that each Scout ties a knot at least two or three times.

Hide the Rabbit ★

Type: Indoor / Traditional / Boy Scout / Small Group / Large Group / Small Area / Quiet
Equipment: none

In Hide the Rabbit, one Scout is given a small object to hide in plain sight. All other Scouts leave the room until the one Scout signals that he is ready. All of the Scouts then come back in and look for the object. When it a Scout finds it, he does not make a commotion or grab the object but instead must quietly walk over to the hider, whisper where the object is, and return to his seat. The other Scouts continue to look for it. When all Scouts have found the object, then the Scout who first discovered the object gets to hide it.

Snake in the Grass ★ ★ ★

Type: Indoor / Outdoor / Active / Small Space / Traditional / Cub Scout
/ Boy Scout / Small Group
Equipment: something to create a defined area

The objective of this game is to tag everyone, turning them into snakes.
To start the game, one player is assigned the role of snake. The snake
must crawl on the ground or on their knees while trying to tag the other
players. When a player is tagged they also become a snake and must
move around on the knees or crawl. Players cannot leave the designated
area or they are out. You can change the difficulty of this game by
changing the size of the area the game is played in or by changing the
starting number of snakes.

North, South, East, West ★ ★ ★

Type: Indoor / Boy Scout / Cub Scout / Small Group / Moderate
Equipment: none

Four corners of the meeting room are designated as North, South, East
and West. The players all begin in the middle of the room. The Scout
leader calls various commands (north, south, east or west) and the
players must rush to that area. The last person to get to that area is out.
Play continues until only one player is left.

Variation 1: Call two locations at a time and have the Scouts rush to
the nearest location. The new calls are Northeast, Northwest, Southeast
and Southwest.

Precision Flying ★ ★

Type: Indoor / Cub Scout / Small Group / Quiet
Equipment: paper to make paper airplanes; a table to place targets on;
cups to be used as targets; markers, tape or rope to make throwing line

Scouts must make paper airplanes (some adult help may be necessary).
A rope or caution tape is placed on the ground about 15 feet away from
the table. Cups are placed on the table and point values are written on

them varying from 5 to 25 points. There should be more cups that are worth 10 to 20 points with a few worth 5 or 25. Scouts line up individually or in small groups behind the line and throw paper airplanes one at a time, aiming to knock cups down to earn the number of points written on them. The group or individual that is able to earn the most points wins. Add more cups for more teams. Do not replace cups once they are knocked down.

I'm Going Hunting   ★ ★

Type: Indoor / Cub Scout / Large Group / Quiet/
Equipment: none

Scouts form a circle. One Scout starts by saying "I'm going hunting and I'm bringing an arrow." The next Scout must say "I'm going hunting and I'm bringing an arrow and ..." adding an item that starts with a B. For example "I'm going hunting and I'm bringing an arrow and a bow." Each Scout after must continue to add to the list using the next letter in the alphabet. When a Scout forgets what he is bringing or uses the wrong letter, they are out and the next person must continue. Things used may not necessarily be things that one would normally bring hunting.

Kim's Game   ★ ★ ★ ★

Type: Indoor / Boy Scout / Cub Scout / Small Group / Quiet / Patrol Competition
Equipment: 15 or more small objects that can be recognized by anybody playing the game, table (optional), Blanket or towel to cover objects with, pencils and paper

Kim's game is a memory game where the group or individual must remember as many objects as possible. Objects are placed randomly on a table and covered. When the group or individuals start watching, the table is uncovered for a short time. Then after time is up, the table is covered and players must write down as many objects as they can remember. If individuals are playing, then fewer objects are usually used and less time is given. When playing with groups, the group compiles a single list as a team. The group or individual that memorizes the most objects wins.

Sleeping Indian ★ ★ ★

Type: Indoor / Boy Scout / Cub Scout / Small Group / Moderate / Traditional
Equipment: blindfold or neckerchief, item to be guarded, seat for Indian (optional)

A Scout is selected to play the "Indian" and he is seated in the center of a circle with the remaining Scouts on the outside. The Indian is blindfolded. He is guarding an item such as a rock or stick or something similar in size which is placed in front of him. Other Scouts must try to steal the item without being heard. When the "Indian" hears a Scout trying to steal the object, he must point at them. When the Scout is pointed at, he must return to the outside of the circle. The first Scout that steals the item without being caught wins.

Subs and Minefields ★ ★ ★

Type: Indoor / Boy Scout / Cub Scout / Large Group / Patrol Competition / Quiet
Equipment: blindfolds or neckerchiefs

One patrol makes a line so that each Scout is side-by-side with another Scout. Each Scout should spread his legs open enough so that the outside of his foot is touching the next Scout's outer foot and place his hands at his sides. The Scouts lined up are blindfolded and become the "mines." Another patrol is the "subs," which must cross the line of mines. They can crawl under or go between the mines to get past the line. If a mine detects a sub, he tries to blow him up by tagging him. If he reaches out with his hand and tags a sub, then the sub is destroyed and the mine continues. If the mine misses, he must place his hand on his knee and cannot use that hand for tagging anymore. Each mine has two tagging chances. If a mine uses up both his chances, he can no longer tag, but also can no longer be crossed by subs. Patrols take turns and whichever gets more subs through the wall of mines successfully wins.

Cat and Mouse ★

Type: Indoor / Traditional / Boy Scout / Small Group / Small Area / Moderate
Equipment: none

This game is best suited for a group that is not too small or not too large. In Cat and Mouse, all but two Scouts form a circle and hold hands. Of the two Scouts not in the circle, one Scout (the Mouse) starts on the inside of the circle, and the other (the Cat) is on the outside. The Scouts forming the circle must attempt to help the Mouse evade the Cat by lifting their arms to let the Mouse run through the circle and lowering their arms to keep the Cat out. Neither the Cat nor Mouse may cross any lowered arms. Additionally, at least one set of arms must be raised at all times. The Mouse can run inside or outside the circle, whichever direction he wants to avoid being tagged. When he is tagged, he becomes the Cat and the Cat picks a new Mouse (not himself). The game is intended for a small space; if playing in too big an area it may be necessary to set boundaries beyond the circle in which the Cat and Mouse cannot go.

Number Call ★ ★ ★

Type: Indoor / Outdoor / Moderate / Cub Scout / Boy Scout / Small Group / Small Space
Equipment: blindfold or neckerchief

A Scout is designated to be "it." This Scout is blindfolded and placed in the center of a circle of the remaining Scouts. The Scouts on the outside of the circle are each assigned numbers. The Scout that is "it" calls two numbers that are assigned to the Scouts in the circle and those two Scouts must switch places without being tagged by the blindfolded Scout. Scouts must go to the spot that the other Scout left from. If they successfully switch places, the Scout that is "it" must call two new numbers and try again, but if he tags someone then they switch roles.

Variation 1: Scouts are assigned numbers in pairs instead of individual numbers.

Gymnasiums or Large Room Games

Indiana Jones ★ ★ ★ ★ ★

Type: Indoor / Outdoor / Boy Scout / Small Group / Large Group /
Large Area / Patrol Competition / Active
Equipment: 5 to 10 pieces of "treasure" (any small item will do, such as
tennis balls or hockey pucks), gym mats, barrels, cones or any items
that can be made into obstacles, dodge balls (about 1 per team member)

This game is essentially a combination of an obstacle course and dodge
ball. The goal is to circumnavigate an obstacle course without getting
hit by a ball. To start, build an obstacle course using whatever materials
might be available. Gym mats or barrels could be positioned so that
players can hide behind them. Mark off a starting line at one end of the
course. On the other end, place a box or define an area to hold the
"Treasure." The treasure can be any items you choose; usually
something small that could be retrieved like, tennis balls or hockey
pucks. There should be about 5 to 10 items that each team must
retrieve.

One team lines up at the starting line, while the second team lines up on
the outside perimeter of the obstacle course with dodge balls. The
throwing team must be outside the perimeter to throw, but may enter
the perimeter to retrieve more balls. On the Scoutmaster's command,
the first team will send their first person through the obstacle course.
They may only bring back one piece of treasure at a time. If they are hit
by a dodge ball, they have "died" and can no longer assist in retrieving
treasure. If they are hit while returning with a piece of treasure, the
treasure stays where they were hit.

The objective of the game is to retrieve the most treasure before all the
players are knocked out. If both teams retrieve all the treasure the
winner is declared based on which team had less casualties or which
team returned all the treasure the fastest. To make this game work
effectively, be sure to establish sidelines for the throwing team to stand
behind. These sidelines must be sufficiently far away so that it is not
too easy to hit players with the ball. The throwing team is allowed to
move up and down the sidelines.

Tom's Dodge Ball ★ ★ ★ ★ ★

Type: Indoor / Outdoor / Active / Boy Scout / Cub Scout / Large Group / Large Area
Equipment: many large Nerf balls or soft dodge balls (depends on size of group)

This game was developed by one of the contributing authors specifically for use with a very large cub pack (more than 120 Scouts). It has been found to be one of the most effective games for a large group of Scouts and works very well with Scouts of all ages. It is best played in a gym but can also be played outside on a sports field. The game begins with all Scouts lined up at one end of the gym and a few leaders or parents lined up along the side wall. The Scouts are on the "running team" and the leaders make up the "throwing team." The leaders are equipped with large size sponge balls. On the Scoutmaster's command all "runners" must run across the room without being hit by the throwers who are throwing sponge balls. Unlike traditional dodge ball where Scouts that are hit are "out" of the game, they become members of the "throwing" team. The last group of Scouts to not get hit are the winners, and they start the next game as the throwing team. The throwers from the previous game become the runners for the next game. This game is quick, highly active and a lot of fun.

Brooklyn Bridge ★ ★ ★

Type: Indoor / Moderate / Small Space / Boy Scout / Small group / Traditional / Patrol Competition
Equipment: kickball, soccer ball or basketball (larger ball works best)

Two teams face each other in parallel lines. Each Scout spreads his feet about 18 inches apart. Scouts from each team alternatively take turns trying to roll the basketball through one of the opposing player's legs. If the ball goes between a Scout's legs, that Scout is out of the game. He can do nothing to stop the ball as it goes "under the Brooklyn Bridge." Last team with a player standing wins. Teams must be a sufficient distance apart to make the game challenging.

Guard the Bucket ★★★★

Type: Indoor Active / Traditional / Boy Scout / Small Group / Small Space / Moderate
Equipment: bucket or milk crate, kickball and staff (any 5 foot walking stick or broom handle will do)

One Scout stands on a bucket in the center of the room with a staff. The rest of the Scouts form a circle around the bucket in about a 10 to 12 foot radius. The objective of the game is for the Scouts in the circle to try to hit the bucket with the ball. The Scout in the middle guards it with the staff. If the ball is deflected, the guard stays. If the ball is deflected off the staff and hits the bucket, it is considered a block and the guard still stays. If a Scout makes a clean hit on the bucket, he takes a turn at guard. Scouts may keep moving the ball around the perimeter, in order to challenge the guard.

Steal-the-Bacon ★★★★

Type: Indoor / Outdoor / Moderate / Small Space / Traditional / Patrol Competition / Cub Scout / Boy Scout / Small Group
Equipment: neckerchief (the bacon)

Make two lines about 10 or 15 feet apart. Line up one patrol on each line and have them face each other, with the "bacon" in the middle. The Scout master will shout out one or more numbers. Each person in a team will be given a number so that they form a pair with someone from the other team. Once the number is called, the two people with that number will race forward and try to bring the bacon back to their team. If the person without the bacon tags the person with the bacon before they get back across their line, then the person that tagged gets a point for their team. If a person succeeds in bringing the bacon back without getting tagged, they get a point for their team. Optional: Each team will rotate and Scouts will get a new number after every few points. The team with the most points wins.

Morse Code Steal-the-Bacon ★★

Type: Indoor / Active / Cub Scout / Boy Scout / Patrol Competition
Equipment: buzzer to signal Morse Code, neckerchief

This game is played the same way as normal steal-the-bacon, but Scouts are assigned Morse code numbers and letters instead of normal numbers. When the buzzer sounds a Scout's Morse Code letter or number, he runs out to steal the bacon. The same steal-the-bacon rules apply.

Variation 1: For added difficulty, use flag semaphore to signal a letter instead of Morse Code

Crows and Cranes ★★★★

Type: Indoor / Outdoor / Traditional / Boy Scout / Small Group / Large Group / Large Area / Moderate
Equipment: none

Scouts are divided into two equal size teams and are designated as Cranes or Crows. Cranes and Crows are then positioned directly next to each other along a center line. Some people prefer the players to be facing each other while some people prefer the Crows and Cranes to be back to back. The game can be played either way. The Scout Leader stands at the end of the line and randomly calls out either Crows or Cranes.

If "Crows" are called, the Cranes must turn and run a short distance across a line to their "base" before the Crows tag them. If any Cranes are tagged, they become Crows, and head to the other side for another round. Likewise, when "Cranes" are called, they must get to their base before being tagged or they become crows. The game is played until all players end up on one side or some time limit is hit.

Variation 1: "Crows and Cranes and Crabs." The rules are the same as Crows and Cranes except when Crabs are called, Scouts are not supposed to move. If they break in either direction, they lose and need to change sides (crows become cranes and vice versa).

Nukem ★ ★ ★ ★ ★

Type: Indoor / Active / Large Space / Cub Scout / Boy Scout / Large Group / Patrol Competition
Equipment: kickball, volleyball or badminton net

The objective of the game is to knock out all the players on the opposing team out by throwing the ball onto their side of the court without anybody catching it. Each side starts with the same number of players and one side starts with the ball. The team with the ball throws it over the net. It must be thrown within the boundaries of the volleyball or badminton court. The opposing team tries to catch the ball before it hits the ground. If they miss the ball, then the team member who missed it or who is closest to where the ball landed is out. If they catch the ball, then they throw it back and continue the game. If any players are taller than the net, they are not allowed to throw the ball in a downward direction. If the ball hits the net or goes out of bounds, then the ball goes to the opposing team. Balls may be bobbled as long as they don't touch the ground. If a Scout touches the ball and then it lands out of bounds, he is out. If multiple people touch and miss a ball they can all be eliminated on a single throw.

Variation 1: When the ball is thrown over the net, players on the opposing team must bounce the ball to at least one other player on their team before they make the final catch. Players can use any part of their body to bounce the ball. The ball still must not touch the ground and if it hits multiple players and then hits the ground, all that touched it are out.

Dodge Ball ★ ★ ★ ★ ★

Type: Indoor / Active / Large Space / Traditional / Patrol Competition / Cub Scout / Boy Scout / Large Group / Small Group
Equipment: dodge balls or foam balls, chalk or tape to make boundaries

The objective of the game is to get all the players on the other team out. The game starts out by dividing the area into halves and lining up the balls on the dividing line. Each team starts behind the outer boundary. When the game starts, both teams must run to the center of the field and grab the balls. Then, they must hit their opponents with the balls to get each other out. When a player is hit by a throw that did not bounce before hitting them, then they are out. Hits to the head are not allowed.

If a player is hit in the head then they are allowed to stay in the game. If it was intentional, then the player who threw it is out. If a player catches a throw, then they are safe and the person who threw it is out. When there are only a few players left, a reduction of boundaries is recommended so players are easier to hit and the game ends faster.

Variation 1: "Medic" is a variation of dodge ball where players can bring teammates back into the game by catching the opponents throw. When a player is out, then they get in a line to get back in. When a teammate catches a ball, the first player in the line can come back in.

Variation 2: "Knock the Block" is a variation of dodge ball where each Scout has a block of wood (or alternatively a bowling pin or 1-liter soda bottle) that they place behind them. Players must knock their opponent's block over to get them out. Balls that bounce or roll are still able to knock the blocks down.

Variation 3: "Pin Dodge Ball" is another variation of dodge ball. The game is set up similarly to regular dodge ball except that each team gets 3 or 4 pins that they can place anywhere on their side of the field. Each team must try to knock their opponents' pins down while protecting their own. Instead of knocking out individual players, a team loses if their pins are knocked down. The game ends when all of one team's pins are knocked down. Players can also accidently knock their own pins down if they are not careful. The team who knocks down the other team's pins first wins.

Virus Ball ★★★★★

Type: Indoor / Boy Scout / Cub Scout / Small Group / Large Group / Large Area / Patrol Competition / Active
Equipment: twenty or more Nerf balls or dodge balls

Divide your group into two teams. Establish a center line in the playing area, and instruct each team that they cannot cross the center line. Line up each team on the opposite ends of the playing area. Place as many "virus" balls of various sizes as possible along the centerline. On signal, the players rush toward the center line and kick the virus balls into the area of the opposing team. The objective is to keep your team's area as free as possible of the "virus." At the end of a pre-determined time, a signal is given to stop play. The team with the fewest "virus" balls in its area wins.

Dead Ant Tag ★ ★ ★

Type: Outdoor / Boy Scout / Large Group / Large Area (needs big boundaries) / Moderate
Equipment: none

Dead Ant Tag begins with one player being "it." This player begins the game as a tagger. When a player is tagged that player must lie down with both hands and feet sticking straight up, like a dead ant. In order for the dead ant to come back to life, four people must tag the dead ant (one on each limb). Once someone has been a dead ant three times they also become "it". At this point, multiple people are "it," making the game challenging.

Infantry Attack ★ ★ ★ ★ ★

Type: Indoor / Outdoor / Active / Boy Scout / Cub Scout / Small Group / Large Group / Small Area
Equipment: minimum 2 Nerf balls or soft dodge balls (depending on group size)

Infantry Attack combines the features of Steal-the-Bacon and Dodge Ball. It can be played in a limited space and with large groups. Multiple games can take place simultaneously. Begin by marking a circular area in the middle of the playing field. Divide players into two teams and have them line up along the marked circle. Each team's players will be assigned a number like in Steal-the-Bacon. Two balls are placed in the circle. When a Scout's number is called, he will race to the middle to try and grab a ball and hit the opposing player with it. The first player to successfully hit the opponent will score a point, and eventually the team with the most points will win. Players on the outside of the circle can attempt to help their team by keeping a ball in play for their teammate to use. Additional balls can be added and two numbers could be called at a time. Players (whose numbers were called) are not allowed to leave the circle for any reason until a point is scored by either team.

Indian Rope Twirl or Helicopter ★ ★ ★

Type: Outdoor / Cub Scout / Boy Scout / Small Group / Active
Equipment: rope about 10 feet in length, caution tape or rope to mark outside boundary

A circle is drawn out using the caution tape. The circle should not be more than 20 feet in diameter. A Scout sits in the center with the rope and spins it over his head. The rope should not be spun above the jumpers' knee level. Other Scouts jump into the circle and then must jump over the rope. If a Scout is hit, then they are out and must leave the circle. If a Scout jumps outside the circle, then they are eliminated. The last person left jumping in the circle becomes the new "Indian" or "helicopter."

Variation 1: Tie a ball to the end of the rope to give it more weight.

Shootout ★ ★ ★ ★

Type: Outdoor / Cub Scout / Boy Scout / Small Group / Active / Patrol Competition
Equipment: small easily thrown balls or larger kickable balls, rope or tape, obstacles (optional), targets (cans, bottles, etc.)

A line is drawn a distance away from the targets. The shooters will be behind this line. Targets are placed between 10 and 30 feet away (varying distances for each target). Younger Scouts may need closer targets and older Scouts may need farther targets. Assign each type of target a point value. Typically larger targets are worth less. Give each team of Scouts a set of balls of varying size and type. Balls may be kicked, rolled or thrown at the targets. After all balls are expended, the points are totaled and the targets are reset for the next team. The same balls must be used for both teams. The team that scores the most points wins. If obstacles are used, place them randomly in the area. Some obstacles may be in front of targets to prevent rolling while others may block above, necessitating rolling.

Field and Outdoor Games

Four Square ★ ★ ★ ★

Type: Outdoor / Active / Small Space / Cub Scout / Boy Scout / Small Group
Equipment: kickball or bouncy ball, a way to designate a playing area of four squares (generally chalk or tape is used)

There are many variations of this game, but the basic concept of the game follows. To set up the game draw a large square about 8x8 ft. divided into four equal sections. Label one box A (Ace), one K (King), one Q (Queen) and one J (Jack). Put one player in each box, usually the least experienced in A and the most experienced in J. The game starts with the ace holding the ball. The ace must bounce the ball once on the ground then hit it underhand into another person's box. After the initial hit, the players may hit the ball in any fashion with their hands. When a player fails to return the ball to another box within one bounce of the ball landing inside their box they are out and sent to the Jack position. The other players move up one box if a space has opened. If the Ace is out, K goes to A, Q goes to K, and J goes to Q. If the King is out then only the Queen and Jack move up. If the Queen is out then the Jack moves up. If the Jack is out, everyone stays where they are. Each round after that is repeated with the A serving the ball. The game may be played with more than 4 players, with the person who is "out" joining a line of extra players with the front person in line becoming the J. The objective is to stay the Ace position the longest.

Variations: Once you get used to the basic game, the Ace can call different playing styles and everyone has to follow the rules of that playing style. Here are some of the many playing styles that can be called by the Ace at the start of a new round:

Categories: When playing categories, the A can call a category at the beginning of each round. This category is any general group that all playing will recognize. The rules are the same except when a player hits the ball they must say a word that fits in the category. For example, for the category trees, players could call oak, maple, elm, or redwood. It requires lots of concentration to do both at the same time.

Treetops: The ball must be hit in an upwards direction above the players heads and does not need to bounce in-between hits.

Double taps: Every time you get the ball you must hit it twice except for the serve. This is good for setting up good spikes and recovering from spikes better.

One-Armed Bandit: Players may only play with one hand (the same hand all round).

Lefty: Players may only hit with their left hand.

Around the World: Players must bounce the ball in the next box in the order; A to K, K to Q, Q to J and J to A. This keeps going until someone gets out.

Body Language: The ball can be bounced to another square using any body part (feet, shoulders, hips, head etc.).

Soccer: The ball can be bounced to another square using any body part except not the hands (feet, shoulders, hip, head etc.).

Tennis: Players need to hit the ball directly next to them- no diagonal passes.

Cement Shoes: Players are not allowed to move their feet.

Electric Fence: You are not allowed to step out of your square. If you do you are out.

Compass Point: Players are not allowed to move their feet, they can only pivot on one foot like a basketball player.

Black Hole: When there are only 2 or 3 players playing the empty square (s) is the black hole and if someone hits it into the square they are out.

Give-and-Go: The person you hit it to must return the ball to you and you must hit it back to them. From there they can send it to any other square.

Thor's Hammer: All strikes must be with both hands together.

Searchlight ★ ★ ★ ★

Type: Indoor / Boy Scout / Cub Scout / Small Group / Quiet
Equipment: flashlight, set of keys

A player is selected to be the searchlight. This player is provided with a flashlight and is blindfolded. He is placed on a chair at one end of the room. The remaining players stand quietly at the other end of the room. The lights are dimmed enough to allow the room to be dark enough to clearly see a flashlight beam. A set of keys is placed somewhere on the floor. Players then compete to quietly grab the keys and return without getting caught. The person with the searchlight attempts to catch the players in the beam. The player who is the searchlight is only allowed to switch the light on and off quickly and he must hold it in position. He is not allowed to swing it round or repeatedly turn it on and off without letting at least some time (about 5 seconds) go between flashes. Any person caught in the beam must quietly exit the game. If someone manages to escape with the keys he is the winner and becomes the searchlight for the next game.

Team Searchlight ★ ★ ★ ★

Type: Indoor / Boy Scout / Cub Scout / Small Group / Patrol Competition / Quiet
Equipment: flashlight, set of keys, blindfold

In the Team version of Searchlight, rather than competing as individuals, a team or patrol tries to secure the keys. The patrol leader quietly taps one player at a time to stealthily approach the keys. Various members of the team attempt to sneak up on the keys until they are successful or until the whole team is eliminated.

Scouts and Indians ★★★★

Type: Indoor / Outdoor / Moderate / Traditional / Boy Scout / Small Group / Large Group / Patrol Competition
Equipment: tape or something appropriate to draw lines

Two lines are drawn (or use tape on the floor) about 10 yards apart. The area behind one line represents the "Indian village" while the space behind the other is the "stockade." The area in between is a "danger zone" for either the Scouts or the Indians; however, each group is "safe" in their own area. Each party makes raids into the neutral territory and captures members of the other team, bringing their bodies across the line and into their areas. Scouts can use any method to capture their opponents but they cannot be too rough either in carrying or attempting to escape. Leaders should use their judgment to ensure that Scouts do not get hurt. Once a Scout is captured, he cannot return to play. At the end of 5 minutes, or if everyone from one team is captured, the game is over and the team or patrol that has captured the most opponents wins.

Tug-of-War ★★★

Type: Indoor / Outdoor / Active / Traditional / Boy Scout / Small Group / Large Group / Patrol Completion
Equipment: extra-large rope with a neckerchief tied to the middle

Classic contest of strength and will between patrols or teams of Scouts. Two teams gather facing each other single file along a drawn out strand of rope. A neckerchief is tied to the middle of the rope. Each Scout grabs the rope and on the Scout leader's signal, each team pulls the rope hoping to draw the neckerchief past a point on their side. The team that is able to draw the neckerchief past a selected point on their side is the winner.

Rope-less Tug-of-War ★★★

Type: Indoor / Outdoor / Active / Traditional / Boy Scout / Small Group / Large Group / Patrol Competition
Equipment: none

No rope? Here's a way to simulate this classic battle. Two Teams form in single file, facing each other arranged in line from tallest (in the middle) to smallest (on the ends). Each Scout clasps his hands across the Scout ahead of him grabbing each other by the wrist. The two lead opposing Scouts in the middle also lock wrists. The team that pulls the other farthest in one minute wins.

Giants, Wizards and Elves ★★★

Type: Outdoor / Boy Scout / Large Group / Large Area (needs big boundaries) / Active
Equipment: pinnies, colored rope, colored ribbon or other identifying marker

Divide the Scouts into three teams: Green Giants, Yellow Wizards and Red Elves. Use some sort of colored identifying marker to designate each team. This could be done with colored pinnies (green, yellow and red), or colored loops made of string or ribbon that could be draped over the head or around the neck. The team identifiers need to be such that they can easily be taken off and put on. You will need at least one of every color identifier for each player, so it is best to have plenty of extras. Define a large playing field and leave spare team identifiers near each of the corner areas of the field. (Don't put them in only one place as it will affect game play. Also it may be helpful to have a circle around these areas that is neutral where players cannot be tagged.)

Giants, Wizards and Elves are each sent to an end area of the field (away from each other) at the start of the game. On the Scout leader's signal, the game begins. Giants must chase the Elves and try to tag them while avoiding Wizards. Elves must chase and try to tag Wizards while avoiding Giants. Wizards must chase and try to tag Giants while avoiding Elves. When a player is tagged they must join forces with the team that tagged them. They must run to one of the designated areas, remove their colored pinnie and put on the pinnie color for the creature they have become. The game ends when all players are on one team / wearing the same color pinnie.

Key: Green Giants beat Red Elves, Red Elves beat Yellow Wizards, Yellow Wizards beat Green Giants.

Nature Scavenger Hunt   ★ ★

Type: Outdoor / Active / Cub Scout / Boy Scout / Small Group / Patrol Competition
Equipment: instruction sheet

Split up Scouts into groups or patrols. Each group is given a list of items that are needed for a potion. (Depending on the situation, the potion could be a magic potion, love potion, healing potion, fire potion, etc.) Make sure the items listed are appropriate to the season and setting. Items might include the leaves of certain trees, a stick, a certain size rock, pine needles, etc. The first patrol to bring back the required items wins. This activity may also be done while hiking.

Flag Pole Raising   ★ ★

Type: Outdoor / Boy Scout / Small Group / Patrol Competition / Active
Equipment per patrol: five poles about 6-feet long and one inch around, including one with the patrol flag attached; eight heavy ropes or cords for lashing; three guy lines each about 17-feet long; three stakes (one for each guy line); hammer to drive in stakes

Patrols line up, each with four poles and a fifth with the patrol flag attached. When the Scout leader yells "go," the Scouts must lash the staves together to make a single flagpole that is about 20 feet long. Then they must secure the three guy lines about two-thirds from the top to support the pole. After the ropes are secure, they raise the flagpole and stake down the guy lines so the pole is straight. When finished, the Scouts assemble in a line at the base of the flag and stand at attention. The first patrol to successfully complete the task wins.

Spud ★★★

Type: Indoor / Outdoor / Active / Large Space / Cub Scout / Boy Scout / Small Group
Equipment: kickball

The game begins with each player receiving a number starting from one. Scouts must remember their assigned number. One person is given the ball and the entire group is instructed to huddle in a bunch in the middle of the playing area. At the beginning of each round, the person with the ball throws the ball straight up while yelling out one of the assigned numbers. Everyone scatters except for the person whose number was called. That person tries to catch the ball. When he controls the ball, he yells "spud." When "spud" is called, everyone must stop where they are, but may turn to face the thrower. Then they cannot move their feet from the position they are in. If players continue running after spud was called, they must go to where they were standing when spud was called. The person who has the ball is then allowed to take three "giant steps" toward any player. He then throws the ball and tries to hit the player. When a player is hit they earn the letter "S," and each additional time they are hit they earn another letter, eventually spelling the word "SPUD." If a player catches the thrown ball, the thrower is assigned a letter. If the thrower misses his target then no letters are awarded and he throws at the beginning of the next round. If someone gets a letter (thrower or catcher), they toss the ball up next and call a new number. Once a player gets all four letters, then they are out of the game. The objective of the game is to get all the other players out. If younger Scouts are playing, adjust the number of steps taken after the initial catch so the game is fair.

Variation 1: Use the "ghost number" or 0 as a number. When 0 is called, everyone must get to the middle and touch the ball. The last player to do that gets a letter. This is very useful when players stay away from the center during the toss.

Variation 2: If you do not want to eliminate players, the game can be played with a time limit and whoever has the least number of letters when time expires wins.

Stretcher Relay ★★★

Type: Indoor / Outdoor / Moderate / Small Space / Large Space / Patrol Competition / Relay games / Boy Scout / Large Group / Small Group
Equipment: large, strong sticks and large blankets for making stretchers

First, have each patrol designate one of the Scouts in the patrol as injured. This Scout needs to be carried away on a stretcher. Have the injured Scout lie on the ground and make sure he doesn't help the rest of his patrol. Then, explain that Scouts will have to make a stretcher out of the materials given and carry the Scout through the course. The course could be as simple as a large circle, but could be complicated and have obstacles. Start the timer after explaining the objective to the Scouts so that the time used in planning and constructing the stretcher is counted along with the amount of time in the course. The objective of the game is to finish the course in the fastest time. Time penalties can be given if the stretcher is dropped or if the injured Scout is further injured.

Variation 1: Don't give the Scouts any materials and let them use materials from the woods or items of clothing to make the stretcher.

Water Boiling ★★★

Type: Outdoor / Boy Scout / Small Group / Large Group / Patrol Competition / Active / Large Wooded Area
Equipment per patrol: two axes, two knives, two matches, a one-quart can without handles filled to one inch from the top with water and with one teaspoon of soap flakes added, wooded area

Patrols must make the water in the pot boil over the edges to win. In order to make the pot boil, Scouts must support the pot using stones or other methods and build a fire underneath. Scouts all start at the fire pit or fire place touching the pot of water. When the Scout leader says "go" the Scouts must gather all materials necessary to build a fire from the woods. Only natural materials can be burned. The Scouts are only given two matches and if they need additional matches, they must run to a designated place some distance away to get more. They can only bring back one match at a time. Scouts may only use the provided material and their clothes to help start the fire. The first patrol to boil the water over wins.

Rope Burning ★★★

Type: Outdoor / Active / Boy Scout / Large Wooded Area / Small Groups / Patrol Competition
Equipment: matches, fire pit, two 18-inch sticks and two 24 inch sticks, rope

This is a classic fire building competition. Scouts must build a fire to burn through rope two-feet off the ground in the shortest amount of time. With a fire ring built, place two 18-inch sticks outside the fire ring opposite to each other. Likewise, place two 24-inch sticks outside the fire ring, across from each other. Tie a rope between the two 18-inch sticks and another between the 24-inch sticks. Scouts are not allowed to build their wood pile higher than 18-inch rope. Sticks also may not touch the 18-inch rope. The 24-inch rope is the rope that needs to be burned through to win. As soon as the instructions are given to the Scouts, time starts. Scouts must collect wood and build a fire that burns the 24-inch rope in the shortest time possible. Scouts may only shield the fire from the wind with their bodies and any natural items found. Scouts can use as many matches as needed to start the fire. The first group to burn through the 24-inch rope wins.

Variation 1: Only one match is given to the patrol. For each additional match, one minute is added to the patrol's time.

British Bull Dog ★★★★★

Type: Indoor / Outdoor / Active / Large Space / Traditional / Patrol / Boy Scout / Large Group
Equipment: none

This is one of the oldest and most traditional Scouting games. Today, the game is more commonly played as a tag game where Scouts need to run across a field or gym without being tagged, but traditionally the game was played with Scouts needing to run across the field without being lifted off the ground. Both versions have the same general rules. One or two Scouts are selected to be "it" and these Scouts go to the center of the playing area. The remaining Scouts, line up on one end of a field or gym. On the leaders signal, Scouts run across the area in an attempt to get to the other side without getting tagged or lifted off the ground. Everyone who is caught joins the group in the middle. The game continues until there are only a few Scouts left. They are declared the winners and are "it" for the next round. This game teaches teamwork as even the smallest Scouts are able to help capture the biggest and most experienced Scouts when everyone works together.

Infiltration ★★★★

Type: Outdoor / Boy Scout / Cub Scout / Large Group / Patrol Competition / Moderate
Equipment: cards or some objects that must be retrieved, marking stakes and rope, two flashlights, two blindfolds

Two Scouts sit in the center of a 75-foot or larger size circle and are blindfolded. These two Scouts are "listeners" who are guarding the cards with their flashlights. The cards should be about eight feet away from the listeners. Patrols organize outside the circle and attempt to steal the cards without being heard. If a Scout enters the circle to steal a card, the listeners can attempt to catch him by hitting him with a beam from the flashlight. If a Scout is caught, he must return to the outside of the circle and try again. If a Scout grabs a card, he must silently return to the outside of the circle without being caught. If a Scout has a card and is caught, he must drop the card where it is and leave the circle. The players who are the listeners are only allowed to switch the light on and off quickly. They are not allowed to swing it round or repeatedly turn it on and off without letting at least some time (about 5 seconds) go between flashes. Once a Scout is outside the circle with the card, his patrol keeps it as a point. The patrol with the most points after 15 minutes wins. Patrols may send in multiple Scouts at a time and they may enter the circle from any point on the perimeter.

Man Hunt ★ ★ ★ ★ ★

Type: Outdoor / Active / Large Space / Traditional / Cub Scout / Boy Scout / Large Group / Small Group
Equipment: a large playing area with lots of obstacles, night time, designated "base"

The objective of Man Hunt is to get to base safely. A single person is the tagger and this person covers his eyes and counts to sixty while at the base. The "runners" all hide in the area while the tagger counts. Players must move at least 50 yards away from base while the tagger counts. When the counter is done he yells, "Ready or not, here I come." The players then try to run to base without being tagged by the tagger. If a player makes it to base safely, then they must yell out a predetermined word or phrase and are safe for the rest of the round. Whoever is tagged first is the tagger for the next round. If nobody is tagged, the last person to get to the base is the new tagger.

Variation 1: "Team Man Hunt" is very similar to Man Hunt except there is more than one person who is "it." Players are put on two teams, the first being the taggers and the other being runners. Typically, there are many runners and few taggers. To begin, taggers must wait at "base" and count to 60. The runners must hide at least 50 yards away from base. When they are done counting, the tagging team must call out "Ready or not, here I come" and try to tag them. The runners try to get to base safely and the taggers try to tag as many runners as they can. When the runners get to base they are safe and cannot be tagged. At the end of the round those tagged become the taggers for the next round. Both those that are safe and those who were taggers in the previous round become runners in the next round.

Variation 2: "Virus Man Hunt" is a variation of Man Hunt. The game starts the same way and runners try to get to base without being tagged. However, if runners are tagged, they join the tagger and help tag other runners. After all runners are either tagged or make it to base, the round is over. The first person tagged starts as the tagger in the next round.

Variation 3: "Infection" is a variation of Virus Man Hunt except there is no "base." The objective is to be the last man standing. One person begins the game as "infected." When he tags someone else, they are also "infected" and join the tagging team. Runners must avoid the infected team for as long as possible. The tagging team will continue to grow until there is only one runner left. The last runner is declared the winner and begins the next round as the "infected" person.

Capture the Flag ★ ★ ★ ★ ★

Type: Active / Large Area / Large Group / Boy Scout / Cub Scout / Patrol Competition / Outdoor / Traditional
Equipment: a way to discern one team from the other and two flags

The objective of the game is to steal the other team's flag and defend your team's flag. To start the game, divide the players into two equal teams and make boundaries. Each team places their flag standing up planted in the ground on their side of the field and sets up a "jail" on their side of the field. Flags must be easily visible. Each side should have similar obstacles and be roughly the same size. The team defending the flag is not allowed within 5 yards of the flag they are defending or the jail they are defending unless the offensive team is within 5 yards of their flag or jail. When a player is on their opponent's side of the field, they may be tagged by any member of the opposing team and are sent to the designated jail. When a player is in jail they may be freed by any member of their team by being tagged. The player that was freed gets a free walk-back to their side of the field and MUST go back to their side of the field before running for the flag. The player who has the free walk-back must put both hands on top of their head and walk directly towards the mid-line. The player who freed them does not get a free walk-back and can be tagged or attempt to capture the flag as usual. Each team is "invincible" on their side of the field. Each team has one "jail break." To use a jail break, a player must go to the center of the field and yell "jail break" loud enough for everyone to hear. Then both teams release all players from their jail and they get free passage back. Players must attempt to cross into their opponents' side of the field and bring the flag back to their side without being tagged by their opponents. If a player is tagged with the flag, the flag is returned to its starting position and the player goes to jail. If all players on a team are jailed, that team loses.

Patrol Capture the Flag ★★★★

Type: Indoor / Outdoor / Active / Large Space / Patrol Competition / Cub Scout / Boy Scout / Large Group /
Equipment: very large playing area, a way to discern the teams, lots of hand-held items for the teams

The objective of the game is to end the game with more "flags" than the other patrols. The game starts off by designating each patrol's side and the boundaries. Each patrol starts the game with the same number of items in a stack on their side of the playing area. The items are the "flags." The items need to be easy to carry and plentiful. If you don't have enough of one given item, you may give each patrol a different kind of item. When the game starts, each patrol can tag anyone from another patrol that is in their territory. When a player is tagged, they must return the flag to the team they took it from, if they have one, and cannot steal another flag. They must walk back to their side of the field before they try to steal flags again. The game runs for 30 minutes and at the end of the 30 minutes each team must count up their flags. Whoever has the most flags wins.

Ice Rescue ★★★★

Type: Outdoor / Active / Cub Scout / Boy Scout / Small Group / Patrol Competition
Equipment: rope of 10 feet in length or greater, tarp to represent "ice," staff or large stick, blanket

This game is used to teach first aid and lifesaving skills, while at the same time creating a scenario for a fun competition. The Scoutmaster presents Scouts with a scenario where a Scout has fallen through the ice and needs to be rescued. Participants must then respond and rescue the Scout before he drowns. They can save the Scout using any number of methods. The game is designed to test the creativity, leadership and teamwork of the contestants.

Place a tarp on the ground to represent the ice. Then instruct a Scout to carelessly walk on the ice and "fall" through. This Scout must lie down and pretend to be drowning. Instruct the rest of the patrol or group to save him using any materials that are available to them. Have a rope and staff lying in an area where they could easily be found and used.

Safe methods of rescue include throwing the rope to the Scout or crawling out on the ice and using the staff to reach the Scout. If a Scout walks on the ice, he is told that he, too, has fallen into the water, and he becomes a second victim. The patrol needs to rescue all victims. Once the victim has been rescued from the water, the patrol or group should provide the necessary first aid for the situation. At a minimum, they should provide treatment for hypothermia and shock. To determine the winner, a judge awards points based on each group's reaction time, ice rescue method, teamwork, leadership, appropriate first aid treatments and Scout spirit. The patrol or group with the most points is the winner.

Variation 1: If at a Klondike Derby, then this game can be incorporated into the Derby. After having the Scout rescued, have the sled team drag the sled across the ice safely.

Variation 2: After the rescue, have the Scouts react to specific first aid situations. These can include frostbite, CPR or any other appropriate first aid scenario.

Retriever ★★★★

Type: Outdoor / Quiet / Cub Scout / Boy Scout / Small Group / Small Area
Equipment: beanbags, hula hoops, tennis balls, blindfold

Scouts must work together in teams of three in order to retrieve objects. One Scout is blindfolded and will be the retriever. Another, called the signaler, can see the playing field but is not allowed to talk. A third, called the instructor, can talk but must stand with his back facing the playing field. The signaler stands in front of the instructor. Only the retriever is allowed on the playing field. Make a playing field where hula hoops, bean bags and tennis balls are spread out. The hula hoops are zones where the retriever cannot go. These can be called lava pits, holes or other similar names. The tennis balls cannot be touched by the retriever. They can be called spiders, poison or other similar names. The bean bags, (called medicine, food or other similar things) must be retrieved to win the game. To get the retriever to collect the items, the signaler must observe the retriever and signal the instructor. The instructor must then give instructions to the retriever based on the signals given. If the retriever enters a hula hoop or touches a tennis ball, he must be sent back to start and the items on the field are shuffled. The team that collects all the bean bags in the shortest amount of time wins.

Spider's Web ★★★★

Type: Outdoor / Moderate / Cub Scout / Boy Scout / Small Group / Small Space
Equipment: two trees that are about 6 to 8 feet apart, lots of rope

To win, Scouts must cross the "spider's web" without touching it and attracting the "spider." To begin, have a neutral group tie the rope between the trees. Have the rope go back and forth between the trees, varying in height. Allow the rope to make openings that Scouts are able to get through, but make the holes as small as possible. Make it difficult to crawl under the "web" and make it near impossible to get over the web.

Start with all members of one group on the same side of the web. When a group tries to cross the web, they can go over, under or through the web without touching it. Once a Scout moves through an opening in the web or underneath it, that opening closes and no other Scouts can go through it. If Scouts are able to get over the web, they may use this path again. If the web is touched at all, the Scouts must restart and the web is reset. Holes that were closed up can be used again. The group that can completely traverse the web in the shortest time wins. If multiple groups are playing, make sure other groups cannot watch the prior groups go and gain an advantage.

Variation 1: If large groups are playing, see which group can get the most members across without touching the web.

Tug-of-War Steal-the-Bacon ★★★★

Type: Outdoor / Active / Cub Scout / Boy Scout / Small Group / Small Space
Equipment: rope, a neckerchief.

This game combines elements of both Steal-the-Bacon and Tug-of-War. Scouts are split into two teams and given numbers that match Scouts on the other team, like Steal-the-Bacon. However, when a Scout's number is called, he must run to a rope and pull it so the neckerchief tied in the center crosses his line like Tug-of-War. Multiple numbers can be called so there are multiple Scouts pulling the rope on both sides. Each time the Scout pulls the neckerchief across his line, his team scores a point. The team with the most points wins.

Ball War   ★ ★ ★ ★

Type: Outdoor / Active / Cub Scout / Boy Scout / Small Group / Large
Space / Patrol Competition
Equipment: many large Nerf balls or soft dodge balls (depends on size
of group), wooded area or fort making materials, a way to discern one
team from the others

This is a cross-country, fort building dodge ball game. Teams can be
made of patrols or can be randomly selected. There can be many teams
or very few, but there must be at least two. This is a two-step game
with a fort building process and a playing process. Scouts are given
time to build a "fort" to use as shelter during the game. Scouts can be
given anywhere from a few minutes to many hours to make forts. Forts
can be made of materials found in the woods or with packs, tent bags
and brought materials. Forts must be made at least 100 yards from any
other fort. Place balls inside each fort. After the fort building time runs
out, the dodge ball phase starts. Scouts can still collect more materials
but are subject to attack from other groups. In the dodge ball stage,
Scouts can defend their fort or move and attack other groups in the
open or in their "forts." Scouts may not enter or touch other teams'
forts for any reason. Once Scouts are hit, then they are out of the game.
The last team standing wins.

Variation 1: If there is snow, make the forts with snow and replace the
balls with snowballs.

Variation 2: This game can have a capture the flag element added in.
After the fort building phase, place flags in front of each fort. Teams
must steal flags from other teams. To capture a flag, a Scout must not
have a ball in his hands. When he takes a flag, he must try to return to
base without being hit. If the Scout carrying the flag is hit with a ball,
he must drop the flag immediately and leave the game. Scouts from any
team may pick up the flag. If the team that owns the flag gets it, they
can move it back in front of their fort but may move it nowhere else. If
the team attempting to steal the flag picks it up, they may continue to
try to steal the flag. In both instances, if the Scout gets hit he must drop
the flag where he was hit and leave the game. If two teams are playing,
the first team to secure their opponent's flag wins. If there are three
teams, the first team to secure a flag wins. If there are four teams, a
team must secure two flags to win. If there are five teams, one must

secure three flags and so on. If a team runs out of players, they lose the game but do not remove their flag as other teams may still capture it.

If there are more than three teams, when a team captures a flag they place the flag in front of their fort. They then have multiple flags. If all of a team's flags have been secured by their opponents, then they are out. If a team has secured an enemy flag and it is in front of their fort, opponents must take and secure both flags to eliminate that team. If a team loses because they run out of players, do not remove their flag as it could still be captured by other teams.

Variation 3: In order to reintroduce players into the game, give each team one "medic." This medic is special because he can bring players back into the game. When players are hit, they must sit where they were hit with their hands on their head and have the medic tag them to bring them back in. Once tagged by the medic, players must run back to their base with their hands on their heads. They cannot pick up any balls or steal any flags until they return to fort. Once players reach their fort, they can play freely again. Medics are still susceptible to attack like any other player. If the medic is hit, they are out and cannot be brought back. Medics can still steal flags and throw balls as well.

Order your Scout Fun Books today!

Scout Riddles

Superior Campfires

The Scout Puzzle & Activity Book

Scout Skits

Scout Jokes

Scoutmaster's Minutes

Scoutmaster's Minutes II

More Scout Skits

Along the Scouting Trail

Campfire Tales

Run-ons and Even More Scout Skits

Scout Games

For an updated list of available books along with current pricing visit: *scoutfunbooks.webs.com*
or find our books on Amazon!

Books are also available on a wholesale basis to qualified Scout Troops, Council Shops, trading posts in quantities of 50 or more. Contact us by email at BoyScoutBooks@aol.com.

Made in America

Made in the USA
Columbia, SC
16 November 2018